How to use this book

Follow the advice, in italics, where given.
Support the children as they read the text that is shaded in cream.
***Praise** the children at every step!*
Detailed guidance is provided in the Read Write Inc. Phonics Handbook.
Activity 8 (Answer the 'questions to read and answer') only appears in Sets 4–7.

8 reading activities

Children:

1 *Practise reading the speed sounds.*
2 *Read the green and red words for the non-fiction text.*
3 *Listen as you read the introduction.*
4 *Discuss the vocabulary check with you.*
5 *Read the non-fiction text.*
6 *Re-read the non-fiction text and discuss the 'questions to talk about'.*
7 *Re-read the non-fiction text with fluency and expression.*
9 *Practise reading the speed words.*

Speed sounds

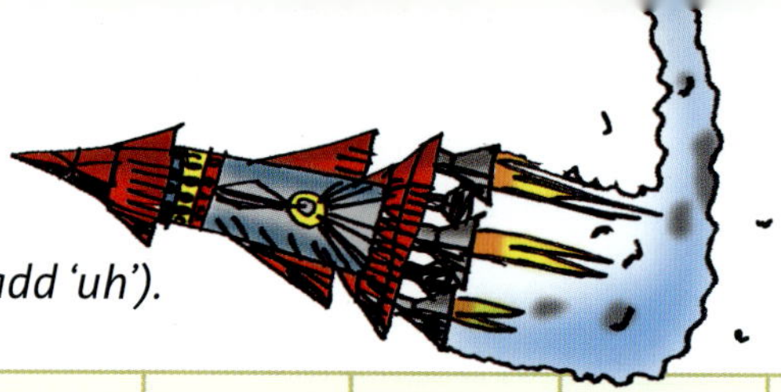

Consonants *Say the pure sounds (do not add 'uh').*

f	l ll	m	n	r	s	v	z s	**sh**	th	ng nk

b	c k **ck**	d	g **gg**	h	j	p	qu	t	w **wh**	x	y	ch tch

Vowels *Say the vowel sound and then the word, e.g. 'a', 'at'.*

at	hen	in	on	up	day	see	high	blow	zoo

Each box contains one sound but sometimes more than one grapheme. Focus graphemes are ***circled****.*

Green words

Read in Fred Talk (pure sounds).

hen	peck	run	mum	slug	shut
shed	when	dish	fox	fresh	scratch

Read in syllables.

coll\` ects → collects

Read the root word first and then with the ending.

fill → fills   help → helps   egg → eggs   hen → hens

Red words

are they the he water

**red for this book only*

Hens

Introduction

What do you know about hens?
Do you know that they lay eggs?
Do you like eating eggs?
In this book we see a boy and his mum looking after hens.

Written by Gill Munton

Vocabulary check

Discuss the meaning (as used in the non-fiction text) after the children have read the word.

	definition
pen	*a place where animals are kept*

Punctuation to note:

Sam	*Capital letters for names*
The They	*Capital letters that start sentences*
.	*Full stop at the end of each sentence*
!	*Exclamation mark*
,	*Comma to show a pause*

Sam's mum has hens.

The hens are in a pen.

They run in the pen.

They scratch in the mud and they peck up insects and slugs.

At ten o'clock, Sam's mum shuts the hens in the shed.

The fox can't get them.

The hens have nests in the shed.

When he gets up, Sam helps Mum with the hens.

He fills the water dish.

He collects
the hens' eggs
from the nests.

Sam has six fresh eggs!

Questions to talk about 

Re-read the page. Read the question to the children. Tell them whether it is a FIND IT *question or* PROVE IT *question.*

FIND IT	**PROVE IT**
✓ *Turn to the page*	✓ *Turn to the page*
✓ *Read the question*	✓ *Read the question*
✓ *Find the answer*	✓ *Find your evidence*
	✓ *Explain why*

Page 10:	FIND IT	*Where are the hens kept?*
Page 11:	FIND IT	*What do the hens do in the mud?*
Page 12:	FIND IT	*Why does Sam's mum put the hens in the shed at night?*
Page 14:	PROVE IT	*What do the hens drink?*
Pages 14–15:	FIND IT	*What does Sam do in the morning?*

Speed words

Children practise reading the words across the rows, down the columns and in and out of order clearly and quickly.

hen	fresh	peck	slug	when
fox	mum	shut	egg	six
run	mud	dish	scratch	get
shed	nest	and	help	fill